Fast Facts About Insects & Spiders

Fast Facts About
BEETLES

by Julia Garstecki

raintree
a Capstone company — publishers for children

Raintree is an imprint of Capstone Global Library Limited, a company incorporated in England and Wales having its registered office at 264 Banbury Road, Oxford, OX2 7DY – Registered company number: 6695582

www.raintree.co.uk
myorders@raintree.co.uk

Edited by Abby Huff
Designed by Kyle Grenz
Original illustrations © Capstone Global Library Limited 2022
Picture research by Jo Miller
Production by Tori Abraham
Originated by Capstone Global Library Ltd

978 1 3982 1328 9 (hardback)
978 1 3982 1327 2 (paperback)

British Library Cataloguing in Publication Data
A full catalogue record for this book is available from the British Library.

Acknowledgements
We would like to thank the following for permission to reproduce photographs: Alamy: Papilio, 18; Dreamstime: Martin Pelanek, 7; Shutterstock: Bildagentur Zoonar GmbH, 19, Dunhill, 20 (right), Ernie Cooper, 8, feathercollector, 10, kingfisher, 5, kossarev56, 15, Mario Saccomano, 17, Nastya22, 9, Protasov AN, 13, Simic Vojislav, cover, Thomas J Ferrugia Jr, 11, tolii_vec, 21, Tomasz Klejdysz, 16, vblinov, 6, Vitaly Zorkin, 20 (top left), zabavina (background), cover and throughout

Printed and bound in India.

Contents

Words in **bold** are in the glossary.

All about beetles

Have you seen a firefly glow? Or counted spots on a ladybird? They are both beetles. A beetle is an **insect**. There are more than 350,000 types of beetles!

Beetles come in many shapes. They come in many sizes. The smallest beetle can fit on the tip of a pin. The biggest is about the size of a person's hand.

Beetles live almost everywhere. Some live in wet rainforests. Others are found in dry deserts. But they don't live where it is very cold.

Beetles make homes in many places. Most live on land. They live on plants or inside wood. Some beetles live in water.

Beetle bodies

Beetles have three body sections. They have two **antennae** on their heads. These feel and smell. Beetles walk on six legs.

legs

antennae

front wing

back wing

Beetles have two pairs of wings. The front wings are hard. This keeps the second pair of wings safe. The back wings are soft. Beetles use them to fly into the air.

Beetles can look very different from each other. The Hercules beetle has a horn. It is used for digging. Diving beetles have hairs on their legs. The hairs help them swim.

Hercules beetle

Many beetles are brown or black. They blend in with the ground. Others are very colourful. They have bright patterns. Some shine in the light.

A beetle's life

A female beetle lays eggs. Each egg hatches a **larva**. The young insect eats. It sheds its skin as it grows. This is called **moulting**. Finally, it becomes a **pupa**.

The pupa is like a shell. The insect does not eat or move. But it is changing. When the insect is ready, it leaves the pupa. It is now an adult.

Beetle life cycle

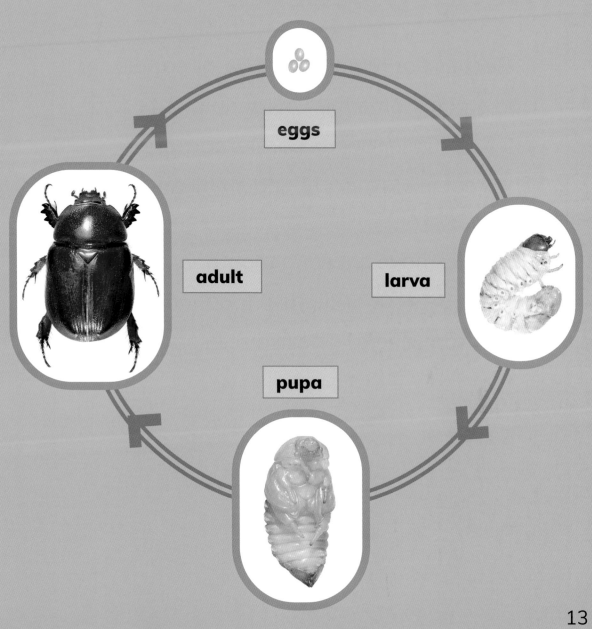

eggs

larva

pupa

adult

Hungry beetles

Beetles eat many things. A lot eat plants and wood. Some feed on dead plants and animals. Other beetles are **predators**. They eat living insects and small animals.

Beetles have chewing mouthparts. These parts cut and crush food. They move from side to side like scissors.

mouthparts

Some beetles cause problems. They are **pests**. They make tiny holes in plants. They eat leaves and roots. The plants may die. This is bad for farmers.

Beetle larvae eating potato plants

Other beetles help. Ladybirds eat insects that hurt plants. Dung beetles eat cow dung. This helps to keep fields clean.

Ladybird eating insects

Fun facts

- The Goliath beetle is one of the biggest insects in the world. Some people keep them as pets.

- People in many places eat beetles. They are often eaten at the larva stage.

Goliath beetle

weevil

- Weevils are a group of beetles with long snouts. Many are pests.

- Beetles are the most common insect. Four out of every ten insects on Earth is a beetle!

Draw a ladybird

What you need:

- paper
- pencil
- red and black felt-tip pens

What to do:

1. Draw a large oval for the body. Add a small half-circle on top for the head.

2. Make a line down the body to show the wings. Draw small circles for the spots.

3. Add two antennae to the head. Add six legs to the body.

4. Colour your ladybird!

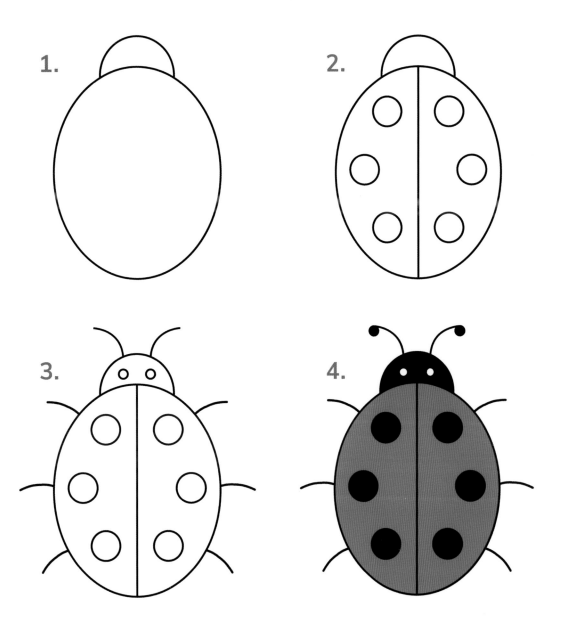

1.

2.

3.

4.

Glossary

antenna feeler on an insect's head used to touch and smell

insect small animal with a hard outer shell, six legs, three body sections and two antennae

larva insect at the stage of its life cycle between an egg and a pupa

moult shed an outer layer of skin; after moulting, a new covering grows

pest animal or insect that causes harm to crops or people's houses

predator animal that hunts other animals for food

pupa insect at the stage of its life cycle between a larva and an adult

Find out more

Books

Insects (Naturetrail), Rachel Firth (Usborne, 2014)

Insects and Spiders: Explore Nature with Fun Facts and Activities (Nature Explorers), DK (DK Children, 2019)

Superstar Insects (Animal Superstars), Louise Spilsbury (Raintree, 2018)

Websites

www.bbc.co.uk/programmes/articles/ 1pB5108szz1wyJjdpBxFS5N/9-facts-about-beetles
Nine fascinating facts about beetles!

www.dkfindout.com/uk/animals-and-nature/insects/ world-beetles
Find out more about the world of beetles.

Index